CHRISTMAS WORSHIP MEDLEYS

— PIANO LEVEL —
LATE INTERMEDIATE/EARLY ADVANCED

ISBN 978-1-4234-5676-6

7777 W. BLUEMOUND RD. P.O. BOX 13819 MILWAUKEE, WI 53213

Visit Hal Leonard Online at
www.halleonard.com

Visit Phillip at
www.phillipkeveren.com

PREFACE

The idea of pairing worship songs with Christmas carols was suggested by my publisher. I was immediately drawn to this concept, and set about selecting songs that worked well together. At times it was lyrical content that inspired the connection, while musical styles made other combinations seem logical. In any case, I found the entire process to be a great pleasure.

Although I am completing this folio of arrangements as spring morphs into summer, I know that "the most wonderful time of the year" will be upon us in no time at all. My prayer is that these settings will help you prepare your heart to worship the King of kings, the true reason for the season.

Merry Christmas!
Phillip Keveren

BIOGRAPHY

Phillip Keveren, a multi-talented keyboard artist and composer, has composed original works in a variety of genres from piano solo to symphonic orchestra. Mr. Keveren gives frequent concerts and workshops for teachers and their students in the United States, Canada, Europe, and Asia. Mr. Keveren holds a B.M. in composition from California State University Northridge and a M.M. in composition from the University of Southern California.

CONTENTS

ANGELS FROM THE REALMS OF GLORY/MAJESTY

Arranged by Phillip Keveren

ANGELS FROM THE REALMS OF GLORY
Words by JAMES MONTGOMERY
Music by HENRY T. SMART

MAJESTY
Words and Music by JACK W. HAYFORD

ANGELS WE HAVE HEARD ON HIGH/ OPEN THE EYES OF MY HEART

Arranged by Phillip Keveren

OPEN THE EYES OF MY HEART
Words and Music by PAUL BALOCHE

ANGELS WE HAVE HEARD ON HIGH

Traditional French Carol

AWAY IN A MANGER/ OH LORD, YOU'RE BEAUTIFUL

Arranged by Phillip Keveren

OH LORD, YOU'RE BEAUTIFUL
Words and Music by KEITH GREEN

AWAY IN A MANGER
Music by JAMES R. MURRAY

COME, THOU LONG-EXPECTED JESUS/ IN CHRIST ALONE

Arranged by Phillip Keveren

Tenderly (♩ = 104)

With pedal

COME, THOU LONG-EXPECTED JESUS
Music by ROWLAND HUGH PRICHARD

IN CHRIST ALONE

Words and Music by KEITH GETTY
and STUART TOWNEND

GOOD CHRISTIAN MEN, REJOICE/ HE IS EXALTED

Arranged by Phillip Keveren

HE IS EXALTED
Words and Music by TWILA PARIS

GOOD CHRISTIAN MEN, REJOICE
14th Century German Melody

HARK! THE HERALD ANGELS SING/ ALL HAIL KING JESUS

Arranged by Phillip Keveren

HARK! THE HERALD ANGELS SING
Music by FELIX MENDELSSOHN-BARTHOLDY

ALL HAIL KING JESUS
Words and Music by DAVE MOODY

IT CAME UPON THE MIDNIGHT CLEAR/ OH HOW HE LOVES YOU AND ME

Arranged by Phillip Keveren

Peacefully, very expressive (♩ = 88)

With pedal

IT CAME UPON THE MIDNIGHT CLEAR
Music by RICHARD STORRS WILLIS

OH HOW HE LOVES YOU AND ME
Words and Music by KURT KAISER

JOY TO THE WORLD/ SHOUT TO THE LORD

Arranged by Phillip Keveren

SHOUT TO THE LORD
Words and Music by DARLENE ZSCHECH

JOY TO THE WORLD
Music by GEORGE FRIDERIC HANDEL
Adapted by LOWELL MASON

O COME, ALL YE FAITHFUL/ HERE I AM TO WORSHIP

Arranged by Phillip Keveren

HERE I AM TO WORSHIP
Words and Music by TIM HUGHES

46

O COME, ALL YE FAITHFUL
Music by JOHN FRANCIS WADE

O COME, O COME, EMMANUEL/ AGNUS DEI

Arranged by Phillip Keveren

O COME, O COME, EMMANUEL
15th Century French Melody

Triumphantly (♩ = 100)

Tempo I

AGNUS DEI
Words and Music by
MICHAEL W. SMITH

With reverence (♩ = 66)

O LITTLE TOWN OF BETHLEHEM/ THERE IS A REDEEMER

Arranged by Phillip Keveren

O LITTLE TOWN OF BETHLEHEM
Music by LEWIS H. REDNER

THERE IS A REDEEMER
Words and Music by MELODY GREEN

WE THREE KINGS OF ORIENT ARE/ WE FALL DOWN

Arranged by Phillip Keveren

WE THREE KINGS OF ORIENT ARE
Music by JOHN H. HOPKINS, JR.

WE FALL DOWN
Words and Music by CHRIS TOMLIN

THE PHILLIP KEVEREN SERIES

PIANO SOLO

00156644	**ABBA for Classical Piano**	$15.99
00311024	**Above All**	$12.99
00311348	**Americana**	$12.99
00198473	**Bach Meets Jazz**	$14.99
00313594	**Bacharach and David**	$15.99
00306412	**The Beatles**	$19.99
00312189	**The Beatles for Classical Piano**	$17.99
00275876	**The Beatles – Recital Suites**	$19.99
00312546	**Best Piano Solos**	$15.99
00156601	**Blessings**	$14.99
00198656	**Blues Classics**	$14.99
00284359	**Broadway Songs with a Classical Flair**	$14.99
00310669	**Broadway's Best**	$16.99
00312106	**Canzone Italiana**	$12.99
00280848	**Carpenters**	$17.99
00310629	**A Celtic Christmas**	$14.99
00310549	**The Celtic Collection**	$14.99
00280571	**Celtic Songs with a Classical Flair**	$12.99
00263362	**Charlie Brown Favorites**	$14.99
00312190	**Christmas at the Movies**	$15.99
00294754	**Christmas Carols with a Classical Flair**	$12.99
00311414	**Christmas Medleys**	$14.99
00236669	**Christmas Praise Hymns**	$12.99
00233788	**Christmas Songs for Classical Piano**	$14.99
00311769	**Christmas Worship Medleys**	$14.99
00310607	**Cinema Classics**	$15.99
00301857	**Circles**	$10.99
00311101	**Classic Wedding Songs**	$12.99
00311292	**Classical Folk**	$10.95
00311083	**Classical Jazz**	$14.99
00137779	**Coldplay for Classical Piano**	$16.99
00311103	**Contemporary Wedding Songs**	$12.99
00348788	**Country Songs with a Classical Flair**	$14.99
00249097	**Disney Recital Suites**	$17.99
00311754	**Disney Songs for Classical Piano**	$17.99
00241379	**Disney Songs for Ragtime Piano**	$17.99
00364812	**The Essential Hymn Anthology**	$34.99
00311881	**Favorite Wedding Songs**	$14.99
00315974	**Fiddlin' at the Piano**	$12.99
00311811	**The Film Score Collection**	$15.99
00269408	**Folksongs with a Classical Flair**	$12.99
00144353	**The Gershwin Collection**	$14.99
00233789	**Golden Scores**	$14.99
00144351	**Gospel Greats**	$14.99
00183566	**The Great American Songbook**	$14.99
00312084	**The Great Melodies**	$14.99
00311157	**Great Standards**	$14.99
00171621	**A Grown-Up Christmas List**	$14.99
00311071	**The Hymn Collection**	$14.99
00311349	**Hymn Medleys**	$14.99
00280705	**Hymns in a Celtic Style**	$14.99
00269407	**Hymns with a Classical Flair**	$14.99
00311249	**Hymns with a Touch of Jazz**	$14.99
00310905	**I Could Sing of Your Love Forever**	$16.99
00310762	**Jingle Jazz**	$15.99
00175310	**Billy Joel for Classical Piano**	$16.99
00126449	**Elton John for Classical Piano**	$19.99
00310839	**Let Freedom Ring!**	$12.99
00238988	**Andrew Lloyd Webber Piano Songbook**	$14.99
00313227	**Andrew Lloyd Webber Solos**	$17.99
00313523	**Mancini Magic**	$16.99
00312113	**More Disney Songs for Classical Piano**	$16.99
00311295	**Motown Hits**	$14.99
00300640	**Piano Calm**	$12.99
00339131	**Piano Calm: Christmas**	$14.99
00346009	**Piano Calm: Prayer**	$14.99
00306870	**Piazzolla Tangos**	$17.99
00386709	**Praise and Worship for Classical Piano**	$14.99
00156645	**Queen for Classical Piano**	$17.99
00310755	**Richard Rodgers Classics**	$17.99
00289545	**Scottish Songs**	$12.99
00119403	**The Sound of Music**	$16.99
00311978	**The Spirituals Collection**	$12.99
00366023	**So Far…**	$14.99
00210445	**Star Wars**	$16.99
00224738	**Symphonic Hymns for Piano**	$14.99
00366022	**Three-Minute Encores**	$16.99
00279673	**Tin Pan Alley**	$12.99
00312112	**Treasured Hymns for Classical Piano**	$15.99
00144926	**The Twelve Keys of Christmas**	$14.99
00278486	**The Who for Classical Piano**	$16.99
00294036	**Worship with a Touch of Jazz**	$14.99
00311911	**Yuletide Jazz**	$19.99

EASY PIANO

00210401	**Adele for Easy Classical Piano**	$17.99
00310610	**African-American Spirituals**	$12.99
00218244	**The Beatles for Easy Classical Piano**	$14.99
00218387	**Catchy Songs for Piano**	$12.99
00310973	**Celtic Dreams**	$12.99
00233686	**Christmas Carols for Easy Classical Piano**	$14.99
00311126	**Christmas Pops**	$16.99
00368199	**Christmas Reflections**	$14.99
00311548	**Classic Pop/Rock Hits**	$14.99
00310769	**A Classical Christmas**	$14.99
00310975	**Classical Movie Themes**	$12.99
00144352	**Disney Songs for Easy Classical Piano**	$14.99
00311093	**Early Rock 'n' Roll**	$14.99
00311997	**Easy Worship Medleys**	$14.99
00289547	**Duke Ellington**	$14.99
00160297	**Folksongs for Easy Classical Piano**	$12.99

00110374	**George Gershwin Classics**	$14.99
00310805	**Gospel Treasures**	$14.99
00306821	**Vince Guaraldi Collection**	$19.99
00160294	**Hymns for Easy Classical Piano**	$14.99
00310798	**Immortal Hymns**	$12.99
00311294	**Jazz Standards**	$12.99
00355474	**Living Hope**	$14.99
00310744	**Love Songs**	$14.99
00233740	**The Most Beautiful Songs for Easy Classical Piano**	$12.99
00220036	**Pop Ballads**	$14.99
00311406	**Pop Gems of the 1950s**	$12.95
00233739	**Pop Standards for Easy Classical Piano**	$12.99
00102887	**A Ragtime Christmas**	$12.99
00311293	**Ragtime Classics**	$14.99
00312028	**Santa Swings**	$14.99
00233688	**Songs from Childhood for Easy Classical Piano**	$12.99
00103258	**Songs of Inspiration**	$14.99
00310840	**Sweet Land of Liberty**	$12.99
00126450	**10,000 Reasons**	$16.99
00310712	**Timeless Praise**	$14.99
00311086	**TV Themes**	$14.99
00310717	**21 Great Classics**	$14.99
00160076	**Waltzes & Polkas for Easy Classical Piano**	$12.99
00145342	**Weekly Worship**	$17.99

BIG-NOTE PIANO

00310838	**Children's Favorite Movie Songs**	$14.99
00346000	**Christmas Movie Magic**	$12.99
00277368	**Classical Favorites**	$12.99
00277370	**Disney Favorites**	$14.99
00310888	**Joy to the World**	$12.99
00310908	**The Nutcracker**	$12.99
00277371	**Star Wars**	$16.99

BEGINNING PIANO SOLOS

00311202	**Awesome God**	$14.99
00310837	**Christian Children's Favorites**	$14.99
00311117	**Christmas Traditions**	$10.99
00311250	**Easy Hymns**	$12.99
00102710	**Everlasting God**	$10.99
00311403	**Jazzy Tunes**	$10.95
00310822	**Kids' Favorites**	$12.99
00367778	**A Magical Christmas**	$14.99
00338175	**Silly Songs for Kids**	$9.99

PIANO DUET

00126452	**The Christmas Variations**	$14.99
00362562	**Classic Piano Duets**	$14.99
00311350	**Classical Theme Duets**	$12.99
00295099	**Gospel Duets**	$12.99
00311544	**Hymn Duets**	$14.99
00311203	**Praise & Worship Duets**	$14.99
00294755	**Sacred Christmas Duets**	$14.99
00119405	**Star Wars**	$16.99
00253545	**Worship Songs for Two**	$12.99

HAL•LEONARD®

Search songlists, more products and place your order from your favorite music retailer at **halleonard.com**

Disney characters and artwork TM & © 2021 Disney LLC

Prices, contents, and availability subject to change without notice.

0422
158